Let's Talk Business

Jason M. Fields

authorHOUSE®

AuthorHouse™
1663 Liberty Drive
Bloomington, IN 47403
www.authorhouse.com
Phone: 1 (800) 839-8640

Published by AuthorHouse   02/02/2016

ISBN: 978-1-5049-7747-0 (sc)
ISBN: 978-1-5049-7746-3 (e)

Print information available on the last page.

Any people depicted in stock imagery provided by Thinkstock are models,
and such images are being used for illustrative purposes only.
Certain stock imagery © Thinkstock.

This book is printed on acid-free paper.

Dedication

This book is dedicated to the young African American Boys and Girls who one day dream of becoming the next Founder, CEO, President, Senior VP of their own Business or empire.

I cannot express in words how much you mean to me, you are the reason I felt the need to write this book! Praying and interceding on your behalf for you to become, grow and operate as children of light, who will one day become the rightful heirs of what we leave here on earth as well as heirs in the kingdom of heaven.

So let this be my gift to you! A BUSINESS Book for Young People Who Are About Their BUSINESS!

"We Go Hard or We Go Home!" "And Just Get It Done!"- Jason M. Fields

Table of Contents

Introduction

What do you think you know about business?

What kind of business do you believe you want?

Do you BELIEVE you can achieve it?

How bad do you WANT IT?

Will anyone or anything stop you?

Why are you going into business?

Will you take notes reading this book?

Will you apply what you learned?

Will you give excuses?

How much money do you have?

Jason M. Fields

Do you think that having money to start your business even matters?

ARE YOU AFRAID?

Do you trust GOD?

After reading this book, answer these questions again!

Chapter 1

What Is The Difference?

So what is the difference?

The difference is the distance between being good and being great! The difference is getting up dusting yourself off after you have been knocked down, and it even goes further than simply being knocked down, it is how many times you will get back up after consistently being knocked down! The difference is having the strength to stand alone, when everyone else is together!

The difference is how you act, and more importantly how you react, to all of life's curve balls that will be thrown in your direction! That is what separates the Players who are in the game versus those who are sitting and taking up space on the bench!

Throughout the history of the world you can see the similarities in all the historical leaders of the past, present and future! They don't make excuses, they accept their fate and they play the cards that they were dealt! They don't complain about problems, rather they continuously seek solutions.

As the young people of our day, you have the choice to become exactly what you want to be. You have the power to create the image of what you want the world to see! You are, in essence created in the image of God, hence you have the ability to act as such! So Do It!!!

To go a little deeper into what kind of traits and characteristics successful people have that are different from unsuccessful people, I have listed a few! The question for you young man or young woman, is simply this, do any of these sound like you, and if so which ones?

Successful People	**Unsuccessful People**
Has a sense of gratitude	Has a sense of entitlement
Forgives people	Holds grudges
Gives praise and credit to others	Only takes credit for the good things
Takes Responsibility	Blames others
Compliments	Criticizes
Reads every day	Watches TV only everyday
Writes in a journal/ or writes things down	Say they write but actually don't
Discusses Ideas and solutions	Talks about people and problems
Likes to see others succeed	Hopes others fail
Open to sharing information and data	Keeps information and data to his/herself
Keeps a list of what they want to accomplish or be	Has no idea, and makes no effort to know what they want to become
Displays joyful attitude	Always angry or complaining
Maintains a To-Do List	Goes with the wind
Constantly learning	Think they know it all
Embraces Change	Fears change and the unknown
Operates from a transformational perspective	Operates from a transaction perspective

This is a starting point to see exactly where and who you are, and whether or not you have some things you should or could improve upon. The difference starts with your attitude and beliefs! The earlier you understand and accept the fact that you are mean to be successful the greater your resolve will be when you come up against trying and chaotic turbulent times in your life.

Grab a hold to these two scriptures and meditate on them daily:

Romans 8:31 New International Version (NIV) [31] What, then, shall we say in response to these things? If God is for us, who can be against us?

Romans 8:37-39 New International Version (NIV) [37] No, in all these things we are more than conquerors through him who loved us. [38] For I am convinced that neither death nor life, neither angels nor demons,[a] neither the present nor the future, nor any powers, [39] neither height nor depth, nor anything else in all creation, will be able to separate us from the love of God that is in Christ Jesus our Lord

Chapter 2

Starting a Business

The greater part of individuals will create one of two mindsets about their work: a representative attitude or an entrepreneur attitude.

Here are a few characteristics of individuals with a representative mindset:

- I work for a paycheck — period.
- There's no compelling reason to give more than I need to, in light of the fact that the organization will exploit me.
- The business is fortunate to have me.
- Somebody is ordered to deal with me.
- I am entitled essentially on the grounds that I work here.
- I just do what I am advised to do.

Trust it or not, even some entrepreneurs have a worker attitude. At the point when a business does not relinquish individual inclination for the benefit of the business, that business has a worker attitude. At the point when a business works a 32-hour week, takes get-aways when due, takes minimal enthusiasm for proceeding with training, and really seizes the chance to close the workplace, that is a worker attitude.

The entrepreneur mindset does not have a place exclusively to entrepreneurs. Workers can build up an entrepreneur mindset that looks good for the business.

Here are a few qualities of the entrepreneur attitude:

- I have a major picture perspective of more noteworthy's benefit I do with my work and understand that wages is the result of the great I do. Basically, my work brings me awesome individual fulfillment.

- When I go the additional mile, I am doing it since it helps the business and the general population we serve.

- I am honored to be a part of this organization.

- It is my obligation to see that my occupation is done to my most prominent ability with each patient consistently. No one can do this for me.

- Entitlement is not a word in my vocabulary. I comprehend that I get compensation for my endeavors, keeping in mind incidental advantages are pleasant, they can vanish if the business is not productive.

- I comprehend that there are times when my very own plan might be hindered for the benefit of the general population we serve.

Most, if not all, businesses would love to have a huge number of staff individuals with an entrepreneur attitude. Such workers are self-roused, don't feel a feeling of privilege, and have the drive to give more than is normal for the benefit of the business.

The Business Owner mindset manages that you comprehend, make inquiries and look for reasonable answers as you set out to begin your own business.

The accompanying is an extract from the SBA site for those of you why should looking begin your own business:

"Why would you like to begin your own Business?

Beginning your own business can be an energizing and a compensating background. It can offer various favorable circumstances, for example, working for yourself, setting your own calendar and bringing home the bacon accomplishing something you appreciate. Be that as it may, turning into an effective business person requires careful arranging, imagination and diligent work.

Consider whether you have the accompanying qualities and abilities usually connected with effective business visionaries:

OK with going out on a limb: Being your own particular manager additionally means you're the one settling on intense choices. Business enterprise includes instability. Do you maintain a strategic distance from instability in life no matter what? On the off chance that yes, then business enterprise may not be the best fit for you. Do you appreciate the rush of going for broke? At that point read on.

Autonomous: Entrepreneurs need to settle on a great deal of choices all alone. On the off chance that you discover you can heed your gut feelings — and you're not perplexed of dismissal occasionally — you could be in route to being a business visionary.

Convincing: You might have the best thought on the planet, however in the event that you can't induce clients, representatives and potential moneylenders or accomplices, you might observe business enterprise to be testing. On the off chance that you appreciate open talking, draw in new individuals easily and discover you make convincing contentions grounded in truths, it's reasonable you're ready to make your thought succeed.

Ready to arrange: As a little entrepreneur, you should arrange everything from leases to contract terms to rates. Cleaned transaction aptitudes will help you spare cash and keep your business running easily.

Innovative: Are you ready to consider new thoughts? Will you envision better approaches to take care of issues? Business visionaries must have the capacity to think inventively. In the event that you have bits of knowledge on the most proficient method to exploit new open doors, enterprise might be a solid match.

Upheld by others: Before you begin a business, it's imperative to have a solid emotionally supportive network set up. You will be compelled to settle on numerous vital choices, particularly in the main months of opening your business. On the off chance that you don't have a bolster system of individuals to offer you, some assistance with considering finding a business coach. A business tutor is somebody who is experienced, effective and willing to give counsel and direction." (https://www.sba.gov/content/enterprise you)

When you are maintaining a fruitful business you might well have the stallions, the yacht, the nation lodge for a considerable length of time away and a speculation portfolio that others can just dream about. Most new organizations begin requiring unreasonable exertion with respect to the proprietor, numerous don't return as much as the wages or pay they were paid until they surrendered to begin their own. Be arranged that as the proprietor you might well be a perfect case for "deferred delight". Representatives are paid a concurred sum each week, proprietors take the great and the terrible as it comes, at any rate until the business creates reliable income.

Beginning your own particular business, putting your complete self into it for perhaps two or three years just to see it sink, bringing your life reserve funds with it sounds like a costly move of the shakers. All things considered, for the ill-equipped it can be.

As a serial entrepreneur and business visionary myself, I felt it was basic for you young fellows and ladies to comprehend and catch wind of the not all that great purposes of being an entrepreneur/business person. The reason I incorporated this is frequently too often, individuals just depict the great things of starting a new business, leaving people, for example, yourself with nor practical desires of precisely what's in store for you! At this point I am certain you have heard numerous more seasoned grown-ups say "In the event that I knew then, what I know now, I would be… ..!" Well, here is my blessing to you, letting you know precisely what some of those awful days will resemble, along these lines when you see them you are not astonished! When you have a thought in the matter of what you're practically going to face you will be more arranged for it over the long haul, and not surrender or quit! Keep in mind nobody ever said it would be simple!!!

20 Things you won't catch wind of being a Business Owner or an Entrepreneur:

"Individuals regularly say that on the off chance that you make it five years in business, you've beaten the chances. What they don't regularly impart to you are the things that happen in those initial five years that add to the high number of individuals whose organizations don't make it.

I'm here to let you know about the individual hardships you're prone to confront in the early phase of business possession. On the off chance that somebody had let me know about these, I may have spared a few tears, kept an early wrinkle and brought down my pulse. These tips are straight from my own encounters beginning different organizations in the previous five years:

Individuals regularly say that on the off chance that you make it five years in business, you've beaten the chances. What they don't frequently impart to you are the things that happen in those initial five years that add to the high number of individuals whose organizations don't make it.

I'm here to let you know about the individual hardships you're prone to confront in the early phase of business proprietorship. On the off chance that somebody had let me know about these, I may have spared a few tears, kept an early wrinkle and brought down my pulse. These tips are straight from my own encounters beginning different organizations in the previous five years:

1. It's forlorn. Regardless of whether you have an accomplice, it can be desolate beginning a business. Your hours will get to be nontraditional, you might be working out of your home or in a little office, and you will center your consideration on work. None of these elements make for an awesome social life right off the bat. Understand this stage is provisional and attempt to set aside a few minutes for individuals who have been there some time recently. They can exhibit that it shows signs of improvement and help you take your psyche off work.

2. Business organizations are hard. Because you are "closest companions" or have "inverse expertise sets" doesn't mean you'll make perfect business accomplices. (I work with my twin sibling, which needs its own manual!) At the end of the day, treat a business association with the admiration you'd give a sentimental organization. Additionally consider a "pre-nup." This ought to be a working understanding (take up some kind of hobby protection arrangement as well, so you can purchase one another out if a casualty happens). Most importantly, be mindful before you focus on a business accomplice. You would prefer not to remove significant time, vitality and cash from the business to separate your organization later.

3. You will be poor for some time. Unless you have a trust reserve, a tremendous bank account, or a rich accomplice, odds are high that you'll be scratching by for some time. Over the long haul, this will help you settle on shrewd money related choices. Be that as it may, while you're in it, it won't be simple. Each choice starts to appear as though it's hued by a monetary lens. You'll understand that won't not have the capacity to go to supper with your companions, take travels or go shopping. You might even cross out your rec center enrollment and magazine memberships (I did). This is every one of the

an extraordinary preparing ground for when you do have cash - ideally you'll recall these intense times and be watchful with your income.

4. It's direction less provocative than you might suspect it is. We see a great deal of pictures of cool business visionaries who became showbiz royalty. The majority of these business famous people experienced tough times yet don't get the chance to discuss them in the media, can't recall that them well, or don't need us to think about the obstacles they hopped. This is similar to the enterprise form of digitally embellishing: it looks incredible on paper, however where it counts, you know it's manufactured.

5. You will question your capacities. Your business will move you. You'll face byways you could have never anticipated. When you lose your first (or tenth) enormous customer, your representatives quit, you separate your accomplice, your accounting report looks troubling, or you can't get financing, you will probably begin to uncertainty yourself. Burrow profound to overcome these circumstances. Eventually, you should be your greatest team promoter.

6. You will think you are the main individual who has experienced this. Give me a chance to be the first to guarantee you, numerous have been through this some time recently. Numerous have fizzled. Ideally they got move down and attempted again with something new. Numerous have succeeded, as well. None of it makes a difference on the off chance that you don't buckle down for it, so continue pushing ahead and discover somebody who's more prepared in business to guide you.

7. You will cry. Individuals regularly contrast their business with youngsters. At the point when your child has a decent day or an awful day, you may wind up crying. It's OK. Feel it and proceed onward.

8. You will never recognize what's in store. Think about the life of your professional the stock exchange. There will be high points and low points, however ideally it will make a positive upward direction after some time. Address the issues, make an arrangement and execute. We are characterized more by how we got up after issues emerge than by how we hurry through the simple times. Napoleon Hill once said, "Most extraordinary individuals have achieved their most noteworthy achievement only one stage past their biggest disappointment." Don't be hesitant to make that next stride.

9. Mistakes are inescapable. On the off chance that you fear botches, you'll never gain ground. Do your best to heed your gut feelings, request direction from trusted sources when you require it, and continue moving. Try not to commit the error of inertia.

10. You will feel confused on occasion. It's difficult to know everything about maintaining your business. When you have legitimate, bookkeeping, IT, land or other inescapable inquiries, motivate referrals to trusted specialists from individuals in your system.

Chapter 3

How to determine if it is a good idea

Is it a smart thought?

Chad Brooks, a senior essayist for "Business News Daily" composed on February 19, 2013 "While great business thoughts are a dime twelve, awesome ones are as basic as a 1965 silver dime.

Only a small amount of new organizations last over two years. So what makes a fruitful endeavor? From uniqueness to the simplicity of scaling the idea up or down, business visionaries say various things ought to be considered when attempting to build up whether a thought is simply great or truly awesome. Here are 10 variables to mull over:

1. Will individuals will pay for it?

It's paying clients who accept a thought and figure out which ones have the best risk for achievement, said Wil Schroter, fellow benefactor and CEO of Fundable.

"A thought is only a thought until you have a paying client connected to it," Schroter said. "Anybody can ruin a basic thought, however nobody can dishonor paying clients."

2. Does it take care of an issue?

Business person and fellow benefactor of the Web outline school, The Starter League, Mike McGee thinks the best business thoughts are those that tackle an issue somehow.

"In the event that there is an issue that influences you, your companions, family, collaborators, and so forth., then the odds are high that it influences individuals you don't know too," McGee said.

3. What's its value point?

Charlie Harary, originator and accomplice of venture firm H3 and Co., said that while there are numerous approaches to tackle issues, incredible business thoughts do it in a way that is less costly than what the business sector will persevere.

"When you have established that you are taking care of a honest to goodness issue scalably, you have to decide not just the worth that it conveys to the world, yet what individuals would pay for that esteem," Harary said. "When you decide the value, then you can evaluate if your answer is business commendable or not."

4. Is it versatile?

As somebody who works with business visionaries every day, specialist and creator Ralph Quintero trusts the colossal business thoughts are ones that can be effectively versatile.

"Would it be able to be systemized, robotized or extended as the enthusiasm for the item develops?" said Quintero, organizer of the media and counseling firm The Great Business Project. "I have seen numerous extraordinary thoughts come up short in light of the fact that the business visionaries behind them never anticipated versatility as needs be."

5. Is it one of a kind?

Kendall Almerico, CEO of the crowdfunding site ClickStartMe.com, says an excess of business visionaries think they are on to an extraordinary thought when their heart begins to pound, their students enlarge and they can't focus on whatever else.

"You know you have an incredible business thought when you quit sweating, return to reality and concentrate enough to Google the idea and discover no one else has ever done it," Almerico said.

6. Does it increase digital footing?

One approach to decide a thought's potential is to make a straightforward site to check whether online buyers are intrigued, said Josh Waller, a hawker at Elastic Inc.

He said the site ought to have an organization name, logo and brief portrayal of the idea. It ought to likewise incorporate a case that says, "Sign up on the holding up rundown — first come, initially served."

"At that point email your contact list requesting that they look at the site, join if intrigued, and offer with other people who may be," Waller said. "In the event that you get a couple of dozen sign-ups in a day, you're presumably onto something, and you as of now have your initial couple of clients to contact."

7. Will merchants be intrigued?

The best pointer of a business' potential achievement is the measure of interest it produces from outside sellers, as per Eugene Lee, president and CEO of ETL Associates.

"On the off chance that fringe organizations are clamoring at your way to pick up a crowd of people, then you can rest guaranteed you are presumably sitting on a lucrative suggestion," Lee said.

8. Is it difficult to copy?

David Handmaker, the CEO of Next Day Flyers, trusts the best business thoughts are the ones that can't without much of a stretch be copied.

"On the off chance that there is an incredible thought and boundaries to section are low, you can make certain imitators will take after," Handmaker said. "New organizations ought to have solid differentiators and/or obstructions, similar to licenses, to avert the opposition."

9. Does it win acknowledgment?

Katie Shea, executive of promoting for OrderGroove, thinks genuinely awesome business thoughts are ostensibly perceived by an outside source, for example, financial specialists, paying clients or the media.

"Acknowledgment from the individuals who are not interlaced with the first thought or business are less one-sided and along these lines more inclined to perceive the distinction between a below average and genuinely uncommon thought," Shea said.

10. Will it last?

Business thoughts that can oblige individuals over a drawn out stretch of time make for the best ventures, as per Ian Aronovich, prime supporter and CEO of GovernmentAuctions.org. Aronovich said business people need to picture their business in two, three and 10 years to figure out whether their item or administration will even now significant.

"Abstain from succumbing to patterns and prevailing fashions, since those can vanish overnight," he said. "In case you're sure your thought will in any case be the solution for your clients' issues and it'll keep on acquiring more income for your business in every one of the years ahead, you have an extraordinary thought to work with." (http://www.businessnewsdaily.com/3969-discovering incredible business-idea.htm

Chapter 4

Business Structure and Types

At the point when starting a business, you should choose what type of business element to set up. Your type of business figures out which wage government form structure you need to document. The most well-known types of business are the sole proprietorship, association, organization, and S enterprise. A Limited Liability Company (LLC) is a generally new business structure permitted by state statute. Legitimate and impose contemplations go into selecting a business structure.

- Sole Proprietorships
- Partnerships
- Corporations
- S Corporations
- Limited Liability Company (LLC)

Sole Proprietorship:

Definition: A business that lawfully has no different presence from its proprietor. Wage and misfortunes are exhausted on the individual's close to home wage assessment form.

The sole proprietorship is the easiest business structure under which one can work a business. The sole proprietorship is not a lawful element. It basically alludes to a man who possesses the business and is by and by in charge of its obligations. A sole proprietorship can work under the name of its proprietor or it can work together under an invented name, for example, Nancy's Nail Salon. The imaginary name is basically an exchange name- - it doesn't make a lawful element separate from the sole proprietor.

The sole proprietorship is a mainstream business structure because of its straightforwardness, simplicity of setup, and ostensible expense. A sole proprietor require just enroll his or her name and secure neighborhood licenses, and the sole proprietor is prepared for business. A particular burden, notwithstanding, is that the proprietor of a sole proprietorship remains by and by at risk for all the business' obligations. Along these lines, if a sole proprietor business keeps running into money related inconvenience, loan bosses can bring claims against the entrepreneur. In the event that such suits are fruitful, the proprietor will need to pay the business obligations with his or her own particular cash.

The proprietor of a sole proprietorship regularly signs contracts in his or her own particular name, in light of the fact that the sole proprietorship has no different character under the law. The sole proprietor will normally have clients compose checks in the proprietor's name, regardless of the fact that the business utilizes an invented name. Sole proprietor proprietors can, and frequently do, coexist individual and business property and assets, something that associations, LLCs and companies can't do. Sole proprietorships frequently have their ledgers for the sake of the proprietor. Sole proprietors need not watch conventions, for example, voting and gatherings connected with the more mind boggling business shapes. Sole proprietorships can bring claims (and can be sued) utilizing the name of the sole proprietor. Numerous organizations start as sole proprietorships and graduate to more mind boggling business frames as the business creates.

Since a sole proprietorship is vague from its proprietor, sole proprietorship tax collection is entirely basic. The wage earned by a sole proprietorship is wage earned by its proprietor. A sole proprietor reports the sole proprietorship salary and/or misfortunes and costs by rounding out and documenting a Schedule C, alongside the standard Form 1040. Your benefits and misfortunes are initially recorded on a tax document called Schedule C, which is documented alongside your 1040. At that point "the primary concern sum" from Schedule C is exchanged to your own expense form. This viewpoint is alluring in light of the fact that business misfortunes you experience the ill effects of different sources.

As a sole proprietor, you should likewise document a Schedule SE with Form 1040. You utilize Schedule SE to figure the amount of independent work charge you owe. You require not pay unemployment charge on yourself, in spite of the fact that you should pay unemployment charge on any representatives of the business. Obviously, you won't appreciate unemployment advantages ought to the business endure.

Sole proprietors are actually subject for all obligations of a sole proprietorship business. We should analyze this all the more nearly in light of the fact that the potential obligation can be disturbing. Accept that a sole proprietor gets cash to work however the business loses its significant client, leaves business, and can't reimburse the advance. The sole proprietor is obligated for the measure of the credit, which can conceivably devour all her own advantages.

Envision a much more dreadful situation: The sole proprietor (or even one her representatives) is included in a business-related mischance in which somebody is harmed or murdered. The subsequent carelessness argument can be brought against the sole proprietor and against her own benefits, for example, her financial balance, her retirement accounts, and even her home.

Consider the former passages precisely before selecting a sole proprietorship as your business structure. Mishaps do happen, and organizations leave business constantly. Any sole proprietorship that endures such a lamentable situation is prone to rapidly turned into a bad dream for its proprietor.

In the event that a sole proprietor is wronged by another gathering, he can acquire a claim his own particular name. Then again, if a partnership or LLC is wronged by another gathering, the element must bring its case under the name of the organization.

The benefits of a sole proprietorship include:

- Owners can build up a sole proprietorship in a split second, effortlessly and cheaply.
- Sole proprietorships convey little, if any, continuous conventions.
- A sole proprietor need not pay unemployment charge on himself or herself (in spite of the fact that he or she should pay unemployment charge on workers).
- Owners might uninhibitedly blend business or individual resources.

The drawbacks of a sole proprietorship include:

- Owners are liable to boundless individual obligation for the obligations, misfortunes and liabilities of the business.
- Owners can't raise capital by offering an enthusiasm for the business.
- Sole proprietorships once in a while survive the demise or insufficiency of their proprietors thus don't hold esteem.

One of the considerable elements of a sole proprietorship is the effortlessness of development. Minimal more than purchasing and offering merchandise or administrations is required. Truth be told, no formal documenting or occasion is required to frame a sole proprietorship; it is a status that arises automatically from one's business activity.

Partnership:

Definition: An authoritative document of business operation between two or more people who offer administration and benefits. The central government perceives a few sorts of organizations. The two most regular are general and constrained organizations.

In the event that your business will be claimed and worked by a few people, you'll need to examine organizing your business as an organization. Organizations come in two assortments: general associations and constrained associations. In a general association, the accomplices deal with the organization and expect obligation regarding the association's obligations and different commitments. A restricted organization has both general and constrained accomplices. The general accomplices own and work the business and expect risk for the organization, while the constrained accomplices serve as financial specialists just; they have no power over the organization and are not subject to the same liabilities as the general accomplices.

Unless you hope to have numerous latent financial specialists, constrained organizations are for the most part not the best decision for another business in view of all the required filings and regulatory complexities. In the event that you have two or more accomplices who need to be effectively included, a general association would be much less demanding to shape.

One of the real points of interest of an organization is the duty treatment it appreciates. An association doesn't pay charge on its pay however "goes through" any benefits or misfortunes to the individual accomplices. At duty time, the association must document an expense (Form 1065) that reports its pay and misfortune to the IRS. Moreover, every accomplice reports his or her offer of salary and misfortune on Schedule K-1 of Form 1065.

Individual risk is a noteworthy concern on the off chance that you utilize a general organization to structure your business. Like sole proprietors, general accomplices are by and by at risk for the association's commitments and obligations. Every broad accomplice can follow up in the interest of the organization, take out advances and settle on choices that will influence and be tying on every one of the accomplices (if the association understanding grants). Remember that associations are likewise more costly to set up than sole proprietorships since they require more legitimate and bookkeeping administrations.

In the event that you choose to compose your business as an organization, make sure you draft an association assention that subtle elements how business choices are made, how question are determined and how to handle a buyout. You'll be happy you have this understanding if for reasons unknown you keep running into troubles with one of the accomplices or in the event that somebody needs out of the course of action.

The assention ought to address the motivation behind the business and the power and obligation of every accomplice. It's a smart thought to counsel a lawyer experienced with little organizations for help in drafting the understanding. Here are some different issues you'll need the consent to address:

- How will the proprietorship hobby be shared? It's a bit much, for instance, for two proprietors to similarly share possession and power. Be that as it may, in the event that you choose to do it, ensure the extent is expressed unmistakably in the understanding.
- How will choices be made? It's a smart thought to build up voting rights on the off chance that a noteworthy contradiction emerges. At the point when only two accomplices claim the business 50-50, there's the likelihood of a stop. To maintain a strategic distance from this, a few organizations give ahead of time to a third accomplice, a trusted partner who might possess just 1 percent of the business however whose vote can break a tie.

- When one accomplice pulls back, in what capacity will the price tag be resolved? One plausibility is to concur on an impartial outsider, for example, your broker or bookkeeper, to discover an appraiser to decide the cost of the association interest.
- If an accomplice pulls back from the organization, when will the cash be paid? Contingent upon the association understanding, you can concur that the cash be paid more than three, five or 10 years, with premium. You would prefer not to be hit with an income emergency if the whole cost must be paid on the spot.

Corporation:

Definition: An authoritative document of business operation between two or more people who offer administration and benefits. The government perceives a few sorts of associations. The two most basic are C-Corp and S-Corp organizations.

On the off chance that your business will be possessed and worked by a few people, you'll need to examine organizing your business as an organization. Organizations come in two assortments: general associations and constrained associations. In a general organization, the accomplices deal with the organization and expect obligation regarding the association's obligations and different commitments. A restricted organization has both general and constrained accomplices. The general accomplices own and work the business and accept risk for the organization, while the restricted accomplices serve as financial specialists just; they have no influence over the organization and are not subject to the same liabilities as the general accomplices.

Unless you hope to have numerous latent speculators, restricted associations are for the most part not the best decision for another business as a result of all the required filings and authoritative complexities. On the off chance that you have two or more accomplices who need to be effectively included, a general association would be much less demanding to frame.

One of the significant focal points of an organization is the duty treatment it appreciates. An organization doesn't pay charge on its pay however "goes through" any benefits or misfortunes to the individual accomplices. At expense time, the organization must record an assessment (Form 1065) that reports its pay and misfortune to the IRS. Moreover, every accomplice reports his or her offer of pay and misfortune on Schedule K-1 of Form 1065.

Individual risk is a noteworthy concern on the off chance that you utilize a general association to structure your business. Like sole proprietors, general accomplices are actually subject for the organization's commitments and obligations. Every broad accomplice can follow up for the association, take out credits and settle on choices that will influence and be tying on every one of the accomplices (if the organization understanding grants). Remember that associations are likewise more costly to build up than sole proprietorships since they require more lawful and bookkeeping administrations.

On the off chance that you choose to compose your business as an organization, make sure you draft an association understanding that points of interest how business choices are made, how question are determined and how to handle a buyout. You'll be happy you have this assention if for reasons unknown you keep running into challenges with one of the accomplices or in the event that somebody needs out of the game plan.

The assention ought to address the reason for the business and the power and obligation of every accomplice. It's a smart thought to counsel a lawyer experienced with little organizations for help in drafting the assention. Here are some different issues you'll need the consent to address:

- How will the proprietorship hobby be shared? It's a bit much, for instance, for two proprietors to just as offer possession and power. Notwithstanding, in the event that you choose to do it, ensure the extent is expressed plainly in the assention.
- How will choices be made? It's a smart thought to set up voting rights in the event that a noteworthy difference emerges. At the point when only two accomplices possess the business 50-50, there's the likelihood of a stop. To dodge this, a few organizations give ahead of time to a third accomplice, a trusted partner who might claim just 1 percent of the business however whose vote can break a tie.
- When one accomplice pulls back, in what capacity will the price tag be resolved? One probability is to concur on an unbiased outsider, for example, your broker or bookkeeper, to discover an appraiser to decide the cost of the organization interest.
- If an accomplice pulls back from the organization, when will the cash be paid? Contingent upon the organization assention, you can concur that the cash be paid more than three, five or 10 years, with premium. You would prefer not to be hit with an income emergency if the whole cost must be paid on the spot on one single amount.

Enterprise:

Definition: A type of business operation that announces the business as a different, legitimate substance guided by a gathering of officers known as the top managerial staff

A corporate structure is maybe the most favorable approach to begin a business in light of the fact that the organization exists as a different substance. As a rule, an enterprise has all the legitimate privileges of a person, aside from the privilege to vote and certain different constraints. Companies are given the privilege to exist by the state that issues their contract. On the off chance that you join in one state to exploit liberal corporate laws however work together in another state, you'll need to petition for "capability" in the state in which you wish to work the business. There's generally a charge that should be paid to qualify to work together in a state.

You can fuse your business by documenting articles of fuse with the fitting organization in your state. Typically, stand out enterprise can have any given name in every state. After joining, stock is issued to the organization's shareholders in return for the money or different resources they move to it consequently for that stock. Once every year, the shareholders choose the governing body, who meet to talk about and guide corporate undertakings anyplace from once per month to once per year.

Every year, the chiefs choose officers, for example, a president, secretary and treasurer to lead the everyday issues of the corporate business. There likewise might be extra officers, for example, VPs, if the executives so choose. Alongside the articles of fuse, the chiefs and shareholders as a rule embrace corporate ordinances that oversee the forces and power of the executives, officers and shareholders.

Indeed, even little, private, proficient companies, for example, a lawful or dental practice, need to stick to the rule that administer an organization. Case in point, upon fuse, basic stock should be appropriated to the shareholders and a directorate chose. In the event that there's stand out individual framing the organization, that individual is the sole shareholder of stock in the partnership and can choose himself or herself to the governing body and some other people that individual esteems suitable.

Partnerships, if legitimately shaped, promoted and worked (counting suitable yearly gatherings of shareholders and chiefs) constrain the risk of their shareholders. Regardless of the fact that the organization is not effective or is held at risk for harms in a claim, the most a shareholder can lose is his or her interest in the stock. The shareholder's close to home resources are not at stake for corporate liabilities.

Companies record Form 1120 with the IRS and pay their own charges. Compensations paid to shareholders who are workers of the organization are deductible. Be that as it may, profits paid to shareholders aren't deductible and along these lines don't diminish the enterprise's expense obligation. An organization must end its duty year on December 31 on the off chance that it gets its pay essentially from individual administrations, (for example, dental consideration, legitimate guiding, business counseling etc) gave by its shareholders.

In the event that the partnership is little, the shareholders ought to get ready and sign a shareholders purchase offer understanding. This agreement gives that if a shareholder bites the dust or needs to offer his or her stock, it should first be offered to the surviving shareholders. It likewise might accommodate a strategy to decide the reasonable value that ought to be paid for those shares. Such assentions are generally financed with extra security to buy the supply of expired shareholders.

On the off chance that an organization is vast and offers its shares to numerous people, it might need to enroll with the Securities and Exchange Commission (SEC) or state administrative bodies. More regular is the partnership with just a couple of shareholders, which can issue its shares with no such enlistment under private offering exceptions. For a little partnership, obligations of the shareholders can be characterized in the corporate minutes, and a shareholder who needs to leave can be suited without numerous lawful bothers. Additionally, until your little partnership has worked effectively for a long time, you will in all likelihood still need to acknowledge individual obligation for any advances made by banks or different loan specialists to your enterprise.

While a few individuals feel that a company improves the picture of a little business, one disservice is the potential twofold tax collection: The Corporation must pay charges on its net pay, and shareholders should likewise pay charges on any profits got from the enterprise. Entrepreneurs regularly build their own compensations to diminish or wipe out corporate benefits and along these lines bring down the likelihood of having those benefits exhausted twice-once to the company and again to the endless supply of profits from the organization.

Subchapter S Corporation:

Definition: A unique type of partnership that permits the assurance of constrained risk yet coordinate move through of benefits and misfortunes

The S company is regularly more alluring to little entrepreneurs than a standard (or C) organization. That is on the grounds that a S organization makes them offer tax cuts and still furnishes entrepreneurs with the risk insurance of a partnership. With a S partnership, salary and misfortunes are gone through to shareholders and included on their individual expense forms. Therefore, there's only one level of government assessment to pay.

A company must meet certain conditions to be qualified for a subchapter S status. To begin with, the partnership must have close to 75 shareholders. In figuring the 75-shareholder confine, a spouse and wife consider one shareholder. Likewise, just the accompanying elements might be shareholders: people, domains, certain trusts, certain associations, charge excluded altruistic associations, and different S organizations.

Limited Liability Company:

Definition: A form of business organization with the liability-shield advantages of a corporation and the flexibility and tax pass-through advantages of a partnership

Numerous states permit a business structure called the Limited Liability Company (LLC). The LLC emerged from entrepreneurs' yearning to embrace a business structure allowing them to work such as a customary association. Their objective was to disperse salary to the accomplices (who reported it on their individual wage expense forms) additionally to shield themselves from individual risk for the business' obligations, as with the corporate business structure. All in all, unless the entrepreneur builds up a different organization, the proprietor and accomplices (if any) accept complete risk for all obligations of the business. Under the LLC rules, be that as it may, an individual isn't in charge of the association's obligation, gave he or she didn't secure them actually, as with a second home loan, an individual Mastercard or by putting individual resources hanging in the balance.

The LLC offers various favorable circumstances over subchapter S organizations. For instance, while S partnerships can issue one and only class of the organization stock, LLCs can offer a few distinct classes with various rights. What's more, S partnerships are constrained to a greatest of 75 individual shareholders (who must be U.S. occupants), while a boundless number of people, organizations, and associations might take an interest in a LLC.

The LLC likewise conveys huge assessment favorable circumstances over the constrained association. Case in point, unless the accomplice in a restricted association accepts a dynamic part, his or her misfortunes are viewed as latent misfortunes and can't be utilized as assessment derivations to balance dynamic salary. Be that as it may, if the accomplice plays a dynamic part in the association's administration, he or she gets to be subject for the company's obligation. It's a conundrum circumstance. business' obligation, and any misfortunes the LLC brings about can be utilized as duty derivations against dynamic wage.

Chapter 5

Multi-Level Marketing

Definition: Multi-level marketing (MLM) is a type of network marketing in which a business is built by creating a tiered network of independent distributors to promote and sell a company's products or services.

Multilevel Marketing Can Be a Good Thing! (Truth be told at the season of composing this book, I am included with three MLM organizations.)

Multilevel promoting (MLM) is an appealing business recommendation to numerous individuals. It offers the chance to wind up included in a framework for conveying items to customers. Not at all like the individual beginning a business starting with no outside help, the multilevel showcasing member has the backing of an immediate offering organization that supplies the items and once in a while offers preparing too.

How MLM Works

As an expert or temporary worker or wholesaler (distinctive organizations call them diverse things) you profit by offering the items to other multilevel showcasing members. In the event that they're not as of now an individual from your MLM Company, you sign them up.

Other than procuring cash off your own particular deals, you likewise win a rate of the salary created by the merchants that you've brought into the system (your down line). Regularly there are rewards for offering specific measures of item or joining a specific number of new individuals; you can procure autos and treks and also money.

Sounds great, isn't that right? Also, being a piece of a well-run MLM business can be a great deal like being an individual from an expansive more distant family.

Fraudulent business models, On the Other Hand...

Shockingly, not each multilevel showcasing opportunity is an authentic business opportunity. Numerous fraudulent business models, fakes intended to part the unwary from their cash, are masked as honest to goodness opportunities.

Like multilevel promoting, fraudulent business models rely on upon enrolling individuals to end up merchants of an item or administration. Like MLM, the fraudulent business model offers the chance to profit by accomplishing so as to join more enlists and certain levels of accomplishment.

The enormous contrast between multilevel promoting and fraudulent business models is that MLM is legitimate in Canada (and the vast majority of the US) and fraudulent business models aren't. Taking an interest in a fraudulent business model is an offense under the Criminal Code of Canada, deserving of up to five years detainment.

Be that as it may, it can be exceptionally troublesome for the individual searching for a business chance to differentiate between an honest to goodness MLM opportunity and a fraudulent business model initially. How would you tell whether it's a real business opportunity or a trick?

Fraudulent business models Have Only One Purpose

The huge contrast between multilevel advertising and a fraudulent business model is standing out the business works. The whole reason for a fraudulent business model is to get your cash and after that utilization you to enroll different suckers (ahem - merchants). The whole motivation behind MLM is to move item. The hypothesis behind MLM is that the bigger the system of wholesalers, the more item the business will have the capacity to offer.

Utilize these inquiries as a corrosive test in case you're at all uncertainty in the matter of whether the open door you're considering is multilevel advertising or a fraudulent business model:

Is It a Pyramid Scheme?

1) Are you required to "contribute" a lot of cash in advance to end up a wholesaler? This speculation solicitation might be camouflaged as a stock charge. Honest to goodness MLM organizations don't require vast start up expenses.

2) If you do need to pay for stock, will the organization purchase back unsold stock? True blue MLM organizations will offer and stick to stock purchase backs for no less than 80% of what you paid.

3) Is there any notice of or consideration paid to a business opportunity for the item or administration? Multilevel promoting relies on upon setting up a business opportunity for the organization's items. In the event that the organization doesn't appear to have any enthusiasm for customer interest for its items, don't join.

4) Is there a bigger number of accentuation on enlistment than on offering the item or administration? Keep in mind, the contrast between multilevel promoting and a fraudulent business model is in the core interest. The fraudulent business model spotlights on quick benefits from marking individuals up and getting their cash. On the off chance that enrollment is by all accounts the center of the arrangement, run.

These next two inquiries will offer you some assistance with determining what the center of the organization is:

5) Is the arrangement composed with the goal that you profit by enlisting new individuals instead of through deals that you make yourself? This is the mark of a fraudulent business model operation.

6) Are you offered commissions for enlisting new individuals? Another fraudulent business model trademark. It's the quantity of individuals why should willing sign up that matters in a fraudulent business model, not the items or administrations being advertised.

Instructions to Protect Yourself

As usual, when you're exploring a potential business opportunity, you'll need to accumulate all the data you can about the MLM Company's items and operations.

Get (and read) composed duplicates of the organization's business writing, strategy for success and/or showcasing arrangement.

Converse with other individuals who have involvement with the multilevel promoting organization and the items, to figure out if the items are really being sold and in the event that they are of high caliber.

Check with the Better Business Bureau to check whether there have been any grievances about the organization.

Furthermore, listen deliberately when you're at that MLM enlistment meeting. Expanded cases for the astounding measures of cash you're going to make ought to set your alerts ringing.

Being a piece of a fruitful multilevel advertising organization can be both gainful and fun, however lamentably, some implied MLM opportunities are really fraudulent business models intended to level both your wallet and your fantasy of maintaining a business.

There is a clothing rundown of multi-level promoting opportunities out there. The way to a fruitful MLM association, is to locate a respectable organization with an item you trust in, and a pay arrangement worth your while. On the off chance that you are occupied with investigating a MLM business opportunity, consider the accompanying. Here are more than 40 different MLM organizations you ought to consider amid your pursuit.

1) **5Linx:** give our clients the most recent in information transfers items, including mobile phones and plans from all major U.S. bearers, satellite TV administration from the business' top suppliers, and the organization's own particular GLOBALINX® VoIP administrations. The organization conveys its items and administrations through a system of autonomous showcasing delegates.

2) **ACN Inc.:** ACN is the biggest direct offering information transfers and key administrations organization on the planet. It has been supported by Donald Trump and included on the Celebrity Apprentice.

3) **AdvoCare:** AdvoCare is a chief wellbeing and health organization offering vitality, weight reduction, sustenance, and games execution items.

4) **Agel Enterprises LLC:** Agel markets another class of suspension gel innovation for wellbeing and health. It disseminates this item through direct deals by means of free deals reps.

5) **Amway:** An immediate offering organization with a wide range of classifications of items such as nourishment, shower and body, magnificence and home items.

6) **Avon:** The world's biggest direct dealer and a main stunner organization, Avon has more than $11 billion in yearly income. Its product offering incorporates excellence, design and home items.

7) **Demarle At Home:** Demarle At Home makers high review silicone-based cookware and molds. It is best known for its mainstream Silpat item. Demarle at Home was created from European's expert cookware organization, Demarle. Its items are utilized routinely on Food Network cooking appears and all through consistent American kitchens.

8) **Discovery Toys:** Discovery Toys offers one of a kind, amazing instructive toys, books, recreations and music and has been utilizing direct offers as a method for circulation for more than three decades.

9) **DoTerra Essential Oils:** Founded in 2008, DoTerra makers and appropriates restorative evaluation crucial oils through a system of autonomous deals reps.

10) **Stream Energy:** Sells power and normal gas vitality through autonomous deals reps. This MLM can just make offers in Texas, Pennsylvania, New Jersey, Maryland and Georgia because of the deregulated vitality market. Built up in 2004.

11) **Forever Living Products:** Forever Living Products International, Inc. is an expansive and worldwide direct offering organization that offers aloe vera and honey bee inferred drinks, beautifiers, nutritious supplements, and individual consideration items in more than 150 nations.

12) **FreeLife:** FreeLife International is a multi-level advertising organization set up in 1995 that supplies dietary supplements. FreeLife is best known for advancing Himalayan Goji Juice, produced using goji berries.

13) **Fuel Freedom International:** Fuel Freedom International is a multi-level advertising organization situated in Altamonte Springs, Florida. Its fundamental item is pills exchange

set apart as MPG-CAPS, which are asserted to enhance mileage, decrease outflows and expansion motor force. These cases are right now under common examination.

14) **Herbalife:** Herbalife International (NYSE: HLF) is a worldwide nourishment, weight reduction and healthy skin organization. The organization was established in 1980 and it utilizes around 4,000 individuals around the world. Herbalife reported net offers of $3.5 billion in 2011. It has a system of 2.1 million autonomous wholesalers.

15) **Isagenix International:** Isagenix International LLC offers items which are said to expel poisons and fat from the body. Established in 2002 and situated in Arizona, it has roughly seven million clients.

16) **Juice Plus:** Juice Plus, a National Safety Associates organization, producers dietary supplements concentrated with foods grown from the ground. This is said to "overcome any issues" for the typical American diet.

17) **LifeVantage:** LifeVantage markets a protected dietary supplement called Protandim, which is said to in a roundabout way expand cancer prevention agent action. The item claims to help with maturing.

18) **Longaberger:** This Company is an American producer of high quality maple wood wicker bin and offers other home and way of life items, including earthenware, fashioned iron, fabric adornments and strength nourishments. The organization demonstrates it has more than 45,000 free deals reps (and its Ohio office building is formed like a mammoth wooden cookout bushel).

19) **Mannatech:** Mannatech is a traded on an open market wellbeing and health organization. It offers around 22 dietary items, two topical items, five healthy skin items, and four weight-administration/wellness items. Mannatech is understood for is item Ambrotose, its "glyconutritional" dietary supplement, which is protected mixes of plant-sourced saccharides. There are almost 350,000 reps.

20) **Market America:** Market America is a top web retailer and item financier organization that uses direct deals with a specific end goal to offer an assortment of items over various markets. It offers items in about each classification. Here is a decent Business Week article revealing some insight into Market America's model.

21) **Mary Kay:** Mary Kay is a settled, billion dollar skincare and restorative organization with more than one billion free deals delegates.

22) **MonaVie:** MonaVie is a drink and Wellness Company dispersing items produced using mixed organic product juice condensed with stop dried acai powder and purée through an autonomous deals system.

23) **Neways:** Neways makes and disperses individual consideration items, healthful supplements, and family cleaning items that are said to be synthetically more secure than contending brands.

24) **Nu Skin Enterprises:** Is a billion dollar traded on an open market system advertising organization which fabricates and offers individual consideration items and dietary supplements. It has a vast business sector in Asia.

25) **PartyLite:** PartyLite is the world's biggest direct vender of candles, light holders and home extras. It utilizes direct deals to market its items and has more than 68,000 reps around the globe.

26) **Primerica:** Primerica is a traded on an open market budgetary administrations system promoting organization. It has around 90,000 free agents, of which 22,000 have a Series-6 Brokerage License. The organization offers life coverage, common assets, paid ahead of time lawful administrations and other budgetary arrangements.

27) **Reliv:** Reliv makers and disseminates healthful supplements. It has roughly 60,000 autonomous deals reps all through the world.

28) **Scentsy Inc.:** Scentsy makers and offers wickless candles and warmers. It guarantees these sorts of candles are much more secure than customary candles. Autonomous deals reps use home gatherings as the primary method for promoting. There are more than 75,000 free deals reps.

29) **Shaklee Corporation:** Shaklee is a secretly held producer and wholesaler of wholesome supplements, weight-administration items, excellence items, and family items.

30) **Sunrider International:** Is a universal MLM which makes wellbeing, excellence, sustenance, and family items. It additionally has a large number of establishment stores in operation. It started in 1982.

31) **Tahitian Noni:** Tahitian Noni is an auxiliary of Morinda Holdings, Inc., is a system showcasing organization that produces and offers "solid" refreshments and skincare got

from the noni plant. This is a privately owned business established in 1996. It has reported it will change its name to Morinda Bioactives.

32) **The Pampered Chef:** A completely possessed auxiliary of Berkshire Hathaway, The Pampered Chef is a worldwide organization that offers a line of kitchen devices, nourishment items, and cookbooks went for planning sustenance in the home with an overall direct deals power of more than 60,000.

33) **Tupperware:** Tupperware creates, fabricates, and appropriates its items universally. It is sold through a system of almost 1.9 million direct deals reps.

34) **Unicity International:** Unicity makes and disperses by means of autonomous deals reps weight reduction items, green tea, nourishment, and individual consideration things. Bios Life and Bios Life Slim are two of their most surely understood items.

35) **USANA Health Sciences:** Usana makes and offers nutritious supplements, vitamins and healthy skin items all around. It is a traded on an open market organization with more than 222,000 free deals reps and more than $500 million in income.

36) **Vector Marketing:** It is the sole wholesaler of Cutco Cutlery Corporation's Cutco Knives. Utilizing free deals reps, it's essential promoting technique is one-on-one in-home exhibitions.

37) **Watkins Inc.:** Watkins Inc. is a producer of wellbeing items, heating items, and other family things which are conveyed in some retail stores, yet for the most part disseminated a free deals power of more than 25,000 reps. This business power offers the items utilizing different routines, including the Internet, individual to individual, exchange appears, party arranging, and gathering pledges.

38) **World Financial Group (WFG):** A completely claimed auxiliary of AEGON, WFG offers venture items, protection and other money related items through a free deals delegate.

39) **XanGo:** Founded in 2002, Xango utilizes a system of free merchants to offer Xango Juice, produced using the mangosteen, and in addition, healthy skin, individual consideration, vitality supplement and nourishing supplement items.

40) **Xocai:** Established in 2005, MXI Corporation fabricates and disseminates by means of free wholesalers "solid chocolate".

41) **Your Travel Biz (YTB):** Founded in 2001 and traded on an open market, YTB utilizes free deals delegates to make proprietor partner sites which offer travel, outings, and cabin.

Disclaimer: This rundown is not the slightest bit an underwriting or formal proposal by Jason M. Fields for a specific organization or individual.

Chapter 6

Basics of Investing

Investing:

Investing is entirely straightforward: Investing means giving your cash for something to do something for you. Basically, it's an alternate approach to consider how to profit. Growing up, the majority of us were taught that you can win a salary just by landing a position and working. What's more, that is precisely what a large portion of us do. There's one major issue with this: in the event that you need more cash, you need to work more hours. Nonetheless, there is a breaking point to how long a day we can function, also the way that having a bundle of cash is unpleasant on the off chance that we don't have the relaxation time to appreciate it

You can't make a copy of yourself to expand your working time, so all things being equal, you have to send an augmentation of yourself - your cash - to work. That way, while you are putting in hours for your boss, or notwithstanding cutting your garden, dozing, perusing the paper or associating with companions, you can likewise be procuring cash somewhere else. Simply, profiting work for you amplifies your gaining potential regardless of whether you get a raise, choose to work extra minutes or search for a higher-paying employment.

There are a wide range of ways you can make a speculation. This incorporates placing cash into stocks, securities, shared assets, or land (among numerous different things), or beginning your own particular business. Some of the time individuals allude to these choices as "venture vehicles," which is simply one more method for saying "an approach to contribute." Each of these vehicles has positives and negatives, which we'll examine in a later segment of this instructional exercise. The fact of the matter is that it doesn't make a difference which technique you decide for contributing your cash, the objective is dependably to give your cash something to do so it wins you an extra benefit. Despite the fact that this is a basic thought, it's the most imperative idea for you to get it.

What Investing Is Not?

Contributing is not betting. Betting so as to bet is putting cash at danger on an indeterminate result with the trust that you may win cash. Part of the disarray in the middle of contributing and betting, be that as it may, might originate from the way a few individuals use speculation vehicles. For instance, it could be contended that purchasing a stock in view of a "hot tip" you heard at the water cooler is basically the same as putting down a wager at a club.

Genuine contributing doesn't happen without some activity on your part. A "genuine" speculator does not just toss his or her cash at any irregular venture; he or she performs intensive investigation and submits capital just when there is a sensible desire of benefit. Yes, there still is danger, and there are no sureties, however contributing is more than just trusting Lady Luck is on your side.

Why Bother Investing?

Clearly, everyone needs more cash. It's really straightforward that individuals contribute in light of the fact that they need to expand their own opportunity, suspicion that all is well and good and capacity to manage the cost of the things they need in life.

Notwithstanding, contributing is turning out to be even more a need. The days when everybody worked the same employment for a long time and afterward resigned to a huge benefits are no more. For normal individuals, contributing is less an accommodating apparatus but rather more the main way they can resign and keep up their present way of life.

Whether you live in the U.S., Canada, or basically some other nation in the industrialized Western world, governments are fixing their belts. Just about regardless, the obligation of getting ready for retirement is moving far from the state and towards the person. There is much open deliberation over how safe our seniority annuity projects will be throughout the following 20, 30 and 50 years. Yet, why abandon it to risk? By arranging ahead you can guarantee money related soundness amid your retirement. (For additional, see Retirement Planning instructional exercise and for Canadians the Registered Retirement Savings Plan (RRSP) instructional exercise.)

Since you have a general thought of what contributing is and why you ought to do it, it's an ideal opportunity to find out about how contributing gives you exploit one of the supernatural occurrences of science: a chance to compound hobby.

Self multiplying dividends:

Albert Einstein called self multiplying dividends "the best scientific revelation ever". We think this is genuine mostly in light of the fact that, dissimilar to the trigonometry or analytics you considered back in secondary school, exacerbating can be connected to ordinary life.

The miracle of exacerbating (infrequently called "progressive accrual") changes your working cash into a cutting edge, very effective salary producing apparatus. Aggravating is the procedure of producing income on a benefit's reinvested profit. To work, it requires two things: the re-speculation of profit and time. The additional time you give your ventures, the more you can quicken the wage capability of your unique speculation, which takes the weight off of you.

To illustrate, we should take a gander at a case:

In the event that you contribute $10,000 today at 6%, you will have $10,600 in one year ($10,000 x 1.06). Presently suppose that as opposed to pull back the $600 picked up from interest, you keep it in there for one more year. On the off chance that you keep on procuring the same rate of 6%, your speculation will develop to $11,236.00 ($10,600 x 1.06) before the second's over year.

Since you reinvested that $600, it cooperates with the first venture, winning you $636, which is $36 more than the earlier year. This smidgen additional might appear like peanuts now, however how about we not overlook that you didn't need to lift a finger to procure that $36. All the more imperatively, this $36 additionally has the ability to gain interest. After the following year, your speculation will be worth $11,910.16 ($11,236 x 1.06). This time you earned $674.16, which is $74.16 more enthusiasm than the main year. This expansion in the sum made every year is exacerbating in real life: enthusiasm acquiring enthusiasm on hobby et cetera. This will proceed the length of you continue reinvesting and acquiring premium.

Beginning Early:

Consider two people, we'll name them Pam and Sam. Both Pam and Sam are the same age. At the point when Pam was 25 she contributed $15,000 at a financing cost of 5.5%. For straightforwardness, we should expect the financing cost was aggravated every year. When Pam achieves 50, she will have $57,200.89 ($15,000 x [1.055^25]) in her financial balance.

Pam's companion, Sam, did not begin contributing until he achieved age 35. Around then, he contributed $15,000 at the same financing cost of 5.5% intensified every year. When Sam achieves age 50, he will have $33,487.15 ($15,000 x [1.055^15]) in his financial balance.

What was the deal? Both Pam and Sam are 50 years of age, however Pam has $23,713.74 ($57,200.89 - $33,487.15) more in her bank account than Sam, despite the fact that he contributed the same measure of cash! By giving her speculation more opportunity to develop, Pam earned a sum of $42,200.89 in premium and Sam earned just $18,487.15.

to pick stocks, a file asset is regularly less expensive than whatever other common asset. (For additional on this, see the Index Investing instructional exercise.)

Melanie doesn't simply stop with her beginning buy. She utilizes a programmed installment arrangement with which she contributes 10% of her paycheck consistently. Contributing a settled sum each and every month makes utilization of dollar expense averaging. By putting in, say, $100 every month (as opposed to a huge sum once per year), Melanie at times purchases when the costs of the units of the asset are higher, and some of the time when costs are lower. At last, the buy costs normal out. The best thing about dollar cost averaging, however, is that it gets Melanie into the propensity for sparing each and every month. Pretty much any asset organization or bank will let you contribute like this with a programmed installment arrangement.

Giving the Concepts something to do. It's as simple as that. It's really basic stuff, really. What's more, notwithstanding the simplicity of setting up a system such as this, it permits Melanie to take after every one of the standards we've been talking about:

1. Her cash is unquestionably being given something to do, and she is turning out to be part proprietor of the 500 greatest organizations in the U.S.

2. With no extra work on her end, she can reinvest all the cash that gets paid out in profits, which permits her to see the advantages of intensifying after some time, considerably all the more so in the event that she sets this asset up in a retirement plan that permits her speculation to develop without being saddled promptly

3. It's simple! This fits Melanie's inclination to maintain a strategic distance from the work of picking stocks. The individuals who would like to add to an eye for stocks, be that as it may, can begin with a file asset and after that in the long run work their way into more dynamic techniques over the long run.

4. A technique like this can be shaped to meet a financial specialist's targets and resource portion. For Melanie's situation, she has a period skyline of over 20 years, so she is happy with being totally in values. In the event that a speculator is not happy with being just in stocks, it's sufficiently simple to purchase a security record reserve. It would even now offer the low expenses of indexing, and permit you to alter your advantage designation.

(Please understand that the above focuses are not intended to give you individual guidance. The purpose of this illustration is to give you a more unmistakable take on how a financial specialist may execute the thoughts examined)

Chapter 7

CrowdFunding

What it is: Crowdfunding is about persuading individuals to each give you a small donation -- $10, $50, $100, maybe more. Once you get thousands of donors, you have some serious cash on hand.

This has all gotten to be conceivable as of late because of an expansion of sites that permit not-for-profits, craftsmen, artists - and yes, organizations - to raise cash. This is the online networking form of raising support.

There are more than 600 crowdfunding stages far and wide, with gathering pledges achieving billions of dollars every year, as indicated by the examination from the firm Massolution.

How it functions: The most well-known sort of crowdfunding raising support is utilizing locales like Kickstarter and Indiegogo assortment, where gifts are looked for consequently for unique prizes. That could mean free item or even an opportunity to be included in outlining the item or administration.

It is additionally conceivable to utilize crowdfunding to gather credits and sovereignty financing. The site LendingClub, for instance, permits individuals to specifically put resources into and acquire from one another, with the case that taking out the managing an account go between signifies "both sides can win" in the exchanges. Eminence financing locales have all the earmarks of being rarer, however the thought is to connection entrepreneurs with speculators who loan cash for an ensured rate of incomes for whatever the business is offering.

The Holy Grail is to offer organization shares or proprietorship stakes in the organization on crowdfunding locales, since it could be similar to a small IPO without the conventional obstacles. Before, this has just been lawful with certify financial specialists, individuals who each have more than $1 million in total assets or more than $200,000 in yearly wage.

The uplifting news is that the Jumpstart Our Business Startups Act of 2012 permits stock to be sold to the overall population over crowdfunding destinations, yet as of mid-2013, the SEC was all the while working out the principles.

Upside: Crowdfunding gives another system to new businesses or early stage organizations prepared to take it to the following level -, for example, revealing an item or administration. Sometime recently, an entrepreneur was liable to the fancies of individual heavenly attendant speculators or bank advance officers. Presently it is conceivable to pitch a strategy for success to the masses.

A fruitful crowdfunding round gives your business required money, as well as makes a base of clients who feel as if they have a stake in the business' prosperity.

Drawback: If you don't have a connecting with story to tell, then you're crowdfunding offered could be a failure. Destinations, for example, Kickstarter don't gather cash until a raising support objective is achieved, so that is still a considerable measure of squandered time that could have been spent doing different things to develop the business.

It could be far more detestable in the event that you meet your objective however then acknowledge you thought little of the amount of cash you required. A business dangers receiving sued on the off chance that it guarantees clients items or advantages consequently for gifts, and after that neglects to convey.

There is likewise a contention to be made that blessed messenger speculators and even bank officers give more than just cash. They give business visionaries required counsel. Entrepreneurs pass up a great opportunity for such mentorship when they overlook conventional speculators and swing to the group.

Here are more components that can better guarantee a fruitful crowdfunding effort:

- Have no less than a little system of excited loved ones giving so as to will to take care of business and encouraging others to give.
- If you're giving out advantages consequently for cash, ensure the advantages are cool.
- Present a genuine strategy for success and a clarification of why the cash will take your undertaking to the following level.
- Demonstrate that you have your own particular skin in the amusement due to the individual assets you have as of now filled the business.
- Include a video pitch and keep it short and brief, with a suggestion to take action.
- PBS incorporates distinctive prizes for various levels of giving; so if you.
- Be arranged to basically live on the internet, staying dynamic on online networking destinations, until the crowdfunding effort has been successful.

1. Crowdfunding advances globalization

Since crowdfunding stages permit individuals from anyplace on the planet to begin a crusade, it opens up a radical new domain of potential outcomes for worldwide organizations. Business visionaries in creating nations, specifically, who might never have generally found the opportunity to propose a business or business sector an item (particularly to individuals in the Western world), are presently on a more level playing field. What's more, crowdfunding stages for metro ventures, natural undertakings, and social equity issues give a chance to individuals to reserve extends that can genuinely affect the world, such as bringing clean water, beginning nearby material organizations and eateries, and advancing equivalent open doors for all.

2. Smaller scale financing is not the same as crowdfunding

Smaller scale financing and miniaturized scale loaning are both once in a while considered crowdfunding, however they are entirely distinctive. Supporters or loaners are paid back over a timeframe dictated by them and the borrower. The most renowned illustration of smaller scale financing is Kiva, which coordinates loan specialists and borrowers from everywhere throughout the world and has an astoundingly high payback rate. Another shared loaning site is Zidisha, which offers a more straightforward association and evacuates the center man, which are the microfinance foundations (MFIs).

3. Crowdfunding advances the triple primary concern

You might have heard that expression some time recently, and it alludes to the triple main concern of manageability in business operations - that is, individuals, benefits, and the planet. The expression was authored by John Elkington in 1997 in his book, Cannibals with Forks: the Triple Bottom Line of 21ˢᵗ Century Business. The fundamental idea is the organization's obligations lie with its partners as opposed to its shareholders. That implies any individual who has a hobby or is some way or another affected by the activities of the organization.

The triple primary concern has been embraced as of late by for-benefits, non-benefits, and government organizations to demonstrate the organization has a more extensive range of deciding achievement. This thought is additionally fundamentally the same to the guidelines of event organizations, who advance business as a force for good.

At last, on the off chance that you need to build the odds of your business thought being supported by a horde of speculators? You ought to have an interesting effort that is energizing and makes individuals need to be a piece of your vision.

Chapter 8

A Franchise Business

On the off chance that purchasing a current business doesn't sound a good fit for you, yet beginning without any preparation sounds somewhat scary, you could be suited for a franchise possession. What is a Franchise - and how would you know in case you're ideal for one? Basically, a franchisee pays a beginning expense and progressing sovereignties to a franchisor. In kind, the franchisee picks up the utilization of a trademark, continuous backing from the franchisor, and the privilege to utilize the franchisor's arrangement of working together and offer its items or administrations.

Notwithstanding a surely understood brand name, purchasing an establishment offers numerous different focal points that aren't accessible to the business person beginning a business starting with no outside help. Maybe the most noteworthy is that you get a demonstrated arrangement of operation and preparing in how to utilize it. New franchisees can stay away from a great deal of the slip-ups start-up business visionaries regularly make on the grounds that the franchisor has effectively consummated every day operations through experimentation.

Legitimate franchisors conduct statistical surveying before offering another outlet, so you'll feel more prominent certainty that there is an interest for the item or administration. Neglecting to do satisfactory statistical surveying is one of the greatest oversights free business people ordinarily make; as a franchisee, it's ruined you. The franchisor likewise gives you an unmistakable photo of the opposition and how to separate yourself from them.

At last, franchisees appreciate the advantage of quality in numbers. You'll pick up from financial aspects of scale in purchasing materials, supplies and administrations, for example, promoting, and in addition in arranging for areas and lease terms. By correlation, autonomous administrators need to arrange all alone, normally getting less ideal terms. A few suppliers won't manage new organizations or will dismiss your business on the grounds that your record isn't sufficiently huge.

Establishment or Business Opportunity?

Business opportunities are less organized than establishments, so the meaning of what constitutes a business opportunity isn't anything but difficult to bind. Generally, a business opportunity is any bundle of merchandise or administrations that empowers the buyer to start a business and in which the dealer speaks to that it will give a promoting or deals arrange for, that a business sector exists for the item or administration, and that the endeavor will be gainful.

Here are other key variables:

- A business opportunity doesn't for the most part highlight the dealer's trademark; purchasers work under his or her own particular name.
- Business opportunities have a tendency to be less costly than establishments and by and large don't charge progressing eminence expenses.
- Business opportunities permit purchasers to continue without any confinements as to geographic business sector and operations.
- Most business opportunity wanders have no proceeding with strong relationship between the merchant and the purchaser; after the introductory bundle is sold, purchasers are all alone.

The Franchisee Satisfaction Award Winners - Best Franchise Opportunities for 2015

There are bunches of "top establishment" rattles off there, however Franchise Business Review's yearly Franchisee Satisfaction Awards are the main establishment positioning taking into account genuine franchisee fulfillment and execution. During the current year's top establishment list, we studied more than 26,000 real establishment proprietors, speaking to more than 350 driving establishment brands, to recognize the Top 50 Franchises in four establishment size classes - Small (under 50 areas), Medium (50 - 99 areas), Large (100 - 249 areas) and Enterprise (250+

Here were 2015 year's Top Franchise Opportunities...

Franchise Name	Industry	Minimum Investment
Sotheby's International Realty	Real Estate	$196,050
Weed Man	Services	$40,000
Visiting Angels	Senior Care	$62,935
Home Instead Senior Care	Senior Care	$100,000
Cruise Planners	Travel	$495
Precision Concrete Cutting	Services	$135,000
Budget Blinds	Home Services	$50,000
Palm Beach Tan	Health & Beauty	$556,695
MaidPro	Cleaning & Maintenance	$30,000
Wild Birds Unlimited	Retail	$104,162
Proforma	Advertising & Sales	$29,500
Sandler Training	Business Services	$82,150
Heaven's Best Carpet Cleaning	Cleaning & Maintenance	$28,900
FASTSIGNS	Business Services	$178,207
Better Homes and Gardens Real Estate	Real Estate	$62,470
Our Town America	Advertising & Sales	$74,800
In Home Pet Services	Pet Services	$9,100
CertaPro Painters	Home Services	$129,000
Christian Brothers Automotive	Automotive	$369,400
Two Men and a Truck	Services	$163,000
Truly Nolen of America	Services	$25,200
Fit4Mom	Fitness	$5,309
Rhea Lana's	Retail	$16,050
HWY 55 Burgers	Food & Beverage	$191,280
National Property Inspections, Inc.	Home Services	$32,900
Window Genie	Services	$89,000

Franchise Name	Industry	Minimum Investment
CarePatrol	Senior Care	$58,000
Men In Kilts Window Cleaning	Services	$43,400
ShelfGenie	Home Services	$70,100
Mosquito Joe	Home Services	$63,850
Home Care Assistance	Senior Care	$150,000
American Poolplayers	Sports & Recreation	$17,080
The Traveling Photo Booth	Services	$27,200
Sir Speedy Printing & Marketing Services	Business Services	$275,000
Amada Senior Care	Senior Care	$92,210
TeamLogic IT	Technology	$80,000
Checkers & Rally's	Food & Beverage	$165,000
Paul Mitchell School	Health & Beauty	$1,021,670
Miracle Method Surface Refinishing	Home Services	$85,000
Aire-Master of America	Cleaning & Maintenance	$19,500
Soccer Shots	Child Services	$16,500
Jan-Pro (master franchisors)	Cleaning & Maintenance	$100,000
Ground Round	Food & Beverage	$600,000
Snap-on Tools	Automotive	$30,164
Homewatch CareGivers	Senior Care	$83,750
CruiseOne	Travel	$4,575
Office Pride Commercial Cleaning Services	Cleaning & Maintenance	$29,900
The Exercise Coach	Fitness	$95,000
Firehouse Subs	Food & Beverage	$169,414
HouseMaster	Home Services	$60,350
A All Animal Control	Services	$10,750
The Goddard School	Education	$701,400
FirstLight HomeCare	Senior Care	$85,281

Franchise Name	Industry	Minimum Investment
Sport Clips, Inc.	Health & Beauty	$156,000
Just Between Friends	Retail	$24,500
HomeVestors of America	Real Estate	$42,300
Sanford Rose Associates	Business Services	$109,350
Synergy HomeCare	Senior Care	$59,025
Pillar To Post Home Inspectors	Home Services	$30,900
LaRosa's Pizzeria	Food & Beverage	$997,000
BrightStar Care	Senior Care	$93,277
Penn Station	Food & Beverage	$294,000
Pinot's Palette	Sports & Recreation	$74,700
WOW 1 DAY PAINTING	Home Services	$94,150
Pinch A Penny	Retail	$250,000
Biggby Coffee	Food & Beverage	$175,850
Young Rembrandts	Child Services	$39,600
Amazing Athletes	Child Services	$38,200
AdvantaClean	Home Services	$92,000
Help-U-Sell Real Estate	Real Estate	$25,000
JumpBunch	Child Services	$28,200
Murphy Business & Financial	Business Services	$45,750
Mathnasium Learning Centers	Education	$99,750
Fitness Revolution	Fitness	$16,278
Best In Class Education Centers	Education	$69,500
Expedia CruiseShipCenters	Travel	$79,500
PIP Printing & Marketing Services	Business Services	$275,000
Anago Cleaning Systems (master franchisors)	Cleaning & Maintenance	$105,000
Right at Home	Senior Care	$76,700

Franchise Name	Industry	Minimum Investment
Surface Specialists Systems	Home Services	$46,000
Linc Service Network	Services	$206,000
Coldwell Banker	Real Estate	$52,470
You've Got MAIDS	Cleaning & Maintenance	$37,999
The Woodhouse Day Spas	Health & Beauty	$392,750
PropertyGuys.com	Real Estate	$45,000
Wingstop	Food & Beverage	$252,621
Bottle & Bottega	Sports & Recreation	$62,950
Kampgrounds of America/ KOA	Sports & Recreation	$17,080
American Prosperity Group	Finance & Tax	$85,000
Tropical Smoothie Cafe	Food & Beverage	$165,940
ActionCOACH	Business Services	$61,250
Learning Express	Retail	$209,500
Leather Medic	Services	$29,000
Preferred Care at Home	Senior Care	$62,500
Chicken Salad Chick	Food & Beverage	$242,000
Qualicare Family Homecare	Senior Care	$73,600
Sit Means Sit	Pet Services	$21,125
Family Fare	Retail	$27,800
YESCO	Business Services	$50,000
Payroll Vault	Finance & Tax	$41,085
360 Clean	Services	$9,500
The Glass Guru	Home Services	$27,190
Auntie Anne's Pretzels	Food & Beverage	$197,875
Baby Boot Camp	Fitness	$3,690
G.J. Gardner Homes	Real Estate	$70,000
Taziki's Mediterranean Cafe	Food & Beverage	$410,000
Big Frog Custom T-Shirts	Retail	$175,000
Auto Appraisal Network	Automotive	$12,000
Line-X	Automotive	$142,750
TGA Premier Golf & Tennis	Child Services	$13,150
Paul Davis Emergency Services	Services	$40,784

Franchise Name	Industry	Minimum Investment
The Little Gym	Child Services	$200,000
Pro Image	Retail	$130,700
Molly Maid	Cleaning & Maintenance	$150,000
DreamMaker Bath & Kitchen	Home Services	$99,791
Tailored Living	Home Services	$85,630
Buildingstars	Cleaning & Maintenance	$2,000
East Coast Wings & Grill	Food & Beverage	$332,500
U.S. Lawns	Services	$48,500
Estrella Insurance	Finance & Tax	$49,000
SuperSlow Zone	Fitness	$119,850
Twin Peaks	Food & Beverage	$1,300,000
Realty ONE Group	Real Estate	$30,000
Critter Control	Services	$12,250
Pop-A-Lock	Services	$30,000
Nothing Bundt Cakes	Food & Beverage	$326,003
Interim HealthCare	Senior Care	$115,500
United Country Real Estate	Real Estate	$15,000
Jet-Black	Services	$46,000
Black Bear Diner	Food & Beverage	$544,300
InXpress	Business Services	$44,700
Oxi Fresh Carpet Cleaning	Cleaning & Maintenance	$33,495
Unishippers	Business Services	$55,000
Mosquito Shield	Home Services	$73,100
Planet Sub	Food & Beverage	$182,500
Paul Davis Restoration	Services	$179,464
THE TUTORING CENTER	Education	$75,000
Padgett Business Services	Finance & Tax	$99,830
McAlister's Deli	Food & Beverage	$177,000
CompuChild	Child Services	$18,300
Happy and Healthy Products, Inc.	Food & Beverage	$45,000

Franchise Name	Industry	Minimum Investment
Crunch Fitness	Fitness	$1,200,000
The HoneyBaked Ham Co. and Cafe	Food & Beverage	$293,300
Hungry Howie's Pizza & Subs	Food & Beverage	$228,000
Toppers Pizza	Food & Beverage	$286,628
Go Mini's	Home Services	$224,440
College Hunks Hauling Junk	Services	$100,000
Orange Theory Fitness	Fitness	$327,600
Precision Door Service	Services	$56,960
Nurse Next Door Home Care Services	Senior Care	$134,600
Welcomemat Services	Advertising & Sales	$49,000
Kid's Closet Connection	Retail	$10,000
Sky Zone Indoor Trampoline Park	Sports & Recreation	$811,000
Viamark Advertising	Advertising & Sales	$37,000
Captain D's	Food & Beverage	$700,000
GolfTEC	Sports & Recreation	$111,475
The Learning Experience	Education	$495,290
FRSTeam	Services	$32,000
Yogurtland	Food & Beverage	$319,800
Boulder Designs	Services	$54,725
You Move Me	Services	$138,000
Showhomes Home Staging	Real Estate	$43,300
ASP - America's Swimming Pool Company	Home Services	$49,200
Fazoli's Restaurants	Food & Beverage	$558,000
Bruegger's Bagels	Food & Beverage	$389,600
Deli Delicious	Food & Beverage	$150,000
Billy Sims Barbecue	Food & Beverage	$169,000
FPC National	Business Services	$93,100

Franchise Name	Industry	Minimum Investment
The Maids	Cleaning & Maintenance	$95,645
Closets By Design	Home Services	$124,900
Color Me Mine	Sports & Recreation	$136,700
Caring Senior Service	Senior Care	$58,035
J.D. Byrider Systems	Automotive	$643,700
Honest-1 Auto Care	Automotive	$169,750
Dick's Wings & Grill	Food & Beverage	$249,000
PostNet	Business Services	$175,045
Fuzzy's Taco Shop	Food & Beverage	$330,260
Chopped Leaf	Food & Beverage	$85,000
Charley's Philly Steaks	Food & Beverage	$152,193
APEX Fun Run	Sports & Recreation	$64,800
Value Place	Hotels	$1,100,000
NYS Collection Eyewear	Retail	$13,580
KidsPark	Sports & Recreation	$172,500
Mr. Rooter Plumbing	Home Services	$68,370
Zinga! Frozen Yogurt	Food & Beverage	$267,000
The Grout Doctor	Home Services	$20,405
ATAX Franchise	Finance & Tax	$41,450
Ascend Collection	Hotels	$1,273,699
Zoup!	Food & Beverage	$327,500
Harcourts USA	Real Estate	$151,000
Engineering For Kids	Child Services	$31,850
Natural Awakenings	Advertising & Sales	$59,700
Bin There Dump That	Services	$150,000
The @WORK Group	Business Services	$75,995
Repicci's Italian Ice	Food & Beverage	$49,500
Snip-Its	Health & Beauty	$120,300
Barberitos	Food & Beverage	$109,800
CareBuilders at Home	Senior Care	$68,750

Franchise Name	Industry	Minimum Investment
Above Grade Level	Education	$50,000
Your Pie	Food & Beverage	$255,000
Liberty Tax Service	Finance & Tax	$56,800
360 Painting	Home Services	$55,625
Mr. Appliance	Home Services	$54,840
Real Property Management	Real Estate	$75,000
101 Mobility	Senior Care	$110,000
Stay at Home	Senior Care	$65,900
Signal 88 Security	Services	$85,000

(Source, The Franchise Business Review: http://topfranchises.franchisebusinessreview.com/franchisee-satisfaction-award-winners-2015/)

Chapter 9

Developing Your Business

When you initially began your business, you presumably did a considerable measure of exploration. You might have looked for assistance from counselors; you might have gotten data from books, magazines and other promptly accessible sources. You put a considerable measure as far as cash, time and sweat value to get your business off the ground. So...now what?

For those of you who have survived startup and manufactured effective organizations, you might be thinking about how to make the following stride and develop your business past its present status. There are various conceivable outcomes, 10 of which we'll diagram here. Picking the best possible one (or ones) for your business will rely on upon the kind of business you claim, your accessible assets, and the amount of cash, time and sweat value you're willing to contribute once more. In case you're prepared to develop, we're prepared to offer assistance.

1. Open another area. This won't not be your best decision for business development, but rather it's recorded first here in light of the fact that that is the thing that regularly rings a bell first for such a large number of business visionaries considering extension. "Physical extension isn't generally the best development answer without cautious research, arranging and number-arranging," says little business speaker, author and specialist Frances McGuckin, who offers the accompanying tips for anybody considering another area:

- Make beyond any doubt you're keeping up a reliable main concern benefit and that you've demonstrated relentless development in the course of recent years.
- Look at the patterns, both financial and customer, for signs on your organization's backbone.

- Make beyond any doubt your managerial frameworks and administration group are phenomenal you'll need them to get another area up and running.
- Prepare a complete marketable strategy for another area.
- Determine where and how you'll get financing.
- Choose your area in light of what's best for your business, not your wallet.

2. Offer your business as an establishment or business opportunity. Bette Fetter, originator and proprietor of Young Rembrandts, an Elgin, Illinois-based drawing program for kids, held up 10 years to start franchising her idea in 2001-yet for Fetter and her spouse, Bill, the timing was great. Bringing up four youthful kids and keeping the business neighborhood was sufficient for the couple until their youngsters became more established and they chose the time had come to grow broadly.

"We picked franchising as the vehicle for development since we needed a working framework that would permit proprietorship with respect to the staff working Young Rembrandts areas in business sectors outside our home domain," says Bette. "At the point when individuals have a personal stake in their work, they appreciate it all the more, convey more to the table and are more effective in general. Franchising is an impeccable framework to finish those objectives."

Streamlining their interior frameworks and showcasing in close-by states offered the couple some assistance with bringing in their initial few franchisees. With seven units added to their repertoire, they then marked on with two national establishment agent firms. Presently with 30 franchisees across the country, they're staying consistent with their vision of relentless development. "Before we started franchising, we were instructing 2,500 youngsters in the Chicago market," says Bette. "Today we show more than 9,000 youngsters across the country, and that number will keep on becoming drastically as we develop our establishment framework."

Bette prompts organizing inside of the establishment group turn into an individual from the International Franchise Association and locate a decent establishment lawyer and in addition a tutor who's been through the establishment process. "You should be interested in developing and extending your vision," Bette says, "yet in the meantime, be a solid pioneer who knows how to keep the key vision in center at all times."

3. Permit your item. This can be a powerful, minimal effort development medium, especially on the off chance that you have an administration item or marked item, notes Larry Bennett, executive of the Larry Friedman International Center for Entrepreneurship at Johnson and Wales University in Providence, Rhode Island. "You can get forthright monies and sovereignties from the proceeded with deals or utilization of your product, name brand, and so on. in the event that it's fruitful," he says. Permitting additionally minimizes your danger and is ease in contrast with the cost of beginning your own particular organization to deliver and offer your image or item.

To discover a permitting accomplice, begin by examining organizations that give items or administrations like yours. "[But] before you set up a meeting or contact any organization, locate an able lawyer who has practical experience in licensed innovation rights," exhorts Bennett. "This is the most ideal approach to minimize the danger of losing control of your administration or item."

4. Structure a union. Conforming yourself to a practically identical kind of business can be a proficient way to deal with expand quickly. The past spring, Jim Labadie purchased a CD course set from a related wellbeing capable, Ryan Lee, on the most capable system to make and offer health information things. It was a move that showed lucrative for Labadie, who at the time was running an upscale individual get ready firm he'd built up in 2001. "What I understood on [Lee's] CDs allowed me to add to my things and structure unions within the business," says Labadie, who now demonstrates business aptitudes to wellbeing specialists by method for a movement of things he made and offers on his Web site, HowToGetMoreClients.com .

Seeing that Labadie had made some by and large invited consequences of his own, Lee agreed to lift Labadie's thing to his long contact once-over of wellness mentors. "That realized a superior than normal measure of offers," says Labadie honestly, he's extended arrangements 500 percent since he made and started offering the things in 2001. "Additionally, there have been other similar associations together I've molded with various mentors and Web regions that offer my things for a commission."

If the considered spending commissions or any of your own money with the end goal of a union makes you uncomfortable, Labadie prompts looking at the all-inclusive strategy: "In case you have to quiet about all the money, you're genuinely shooting yourself in the foot," says the Tampa, Florida, representative. "You need to acclimate to various associations that starting now have courses of action of approaching customers. It's the snappiest way to deal with ato achievement."

5. Expand. Little business specialist McGuckin offers a few thoughts for expanding your item or administration line:

- Sell integral items or administrations
- Teach grown-up instruction or different sorts of classes
- Import or send out yours or others' items
- Become a paid speaker or journalist

"Differentiating is an astounding development system, as it permits you to have numerous floods of wage that can regularly fill occasional voids and, obviously, expand deals and net revenues," says McGuckin, who enhanced from a bookkeeping, assess and counseling business to talking, composing and distributed.

Enhancing was dependably in progress for Darien, Connecticut, business people Rebecca Cutler and Jennifer Krane, inventors of the "raising a racquet" line of maternity tennis wear, dispatched in 2002. "We had constantly wanted to venture into other "topical" packs, steady with our rationalities of adaptability, style, wellbeing and fun," says Cutler. "Once we'd started to set up a steadfast wholesale client base and accomplish some retail mark acknowledgment, we then expanded our item base with two line expansions, 'raising a racquet golf' and 'raising a racquet yoga.'"

Revealing the new lines a year ago permitted the accomplices' present retail outlets to convey a greater amount of their stock. "It likewise expanded our intended interest group and expanded our vicinity in the commercial center, giving us the believability to approach much bigger retailers," notes Cutler, who hopes to twofold their 2003 deals this year and further differentiate the organization's product offerings. "As verification, we've as of late been chosen by Bloomingdale's, A Pea in the Pod and Mimi Maternity."

6. Target different markets. Your present business sector is serving you well. Are there others? You wager. "My different markets are what profit for me," says McGuckin. Electronic and outside rights, business enterprise programs, talking occasions and programming offerings deliver different income streams for McGuckin, from numerous business sectors.

"On the off chance that your purchaser market ranges from adolescents to undergrads, consider where these individuals invest a large portion of their energy," says McGuckin. "Might you be able to acquaint your business with schools, clubs or universities? You could offer rebates to exceptional interest clubs or give a portion of [your profits] to schools and affiliations."

Gen X-ers, elderly people, teenagers, tweens...let your creative energy take you where you should be. At that point take your item to the business sectors that need it.

7. Win an administration contract. "The most ideal path for a little business to develop is to have the central government as a client," composed Rep. Nydia M. Velazquez, positioning Democratic individual from the House Small Business Committee, in August 2003. Did you realize that "The U.S. government is the biggest purchaser of products and administrations on the planet, with aggregate acquisition dollars coming to around $235 billion in 2002 alone??"

Working with your neighborhood SBA and SBDC workplaces and additionally the Service Corps of Retired Executives and your nearby, local or state Economic Development Agency will offer you some assistance with determining the sorts of agreements accessible to you. The U.S. Council of Commerce and the SBA likewise have a Business Matchmaking Program intended to match business people with purchasers. "A considerable lot of tolerance is required in attempting to secure most government contracts," says Johnson and Wales University's Bennett. "Demands for proposition for the most part require a lot of preparation and exploration. In case you're not arranged to take the opportunity to completely consent to RFP terms and conditions, you'll just be squandering your time."

This may seem like a considerable measure of work, yet it could be justified, despite all the trouble: "The great part about winning government contracts," says Bennett, "is that once you've paid some dues and win an offer, you're for the most part not subject to the level of outer rivalry of the outside commercial centers."

8. Converge with or get another business. In 1996, when Mark Fasciano established FatWire, a Mineola, New York, content administration programming organization, he unquestionably couldn't have anticipated what might happen a couple of years after the fact. Pretty much as FatWire was picking up business sector force, the tech downturn hit hard. "We were not able create the development expected to augment the vital associations we'd set up with key industry players," Fasciano says. "Amid this tech "winter," we focused on survival and adjusting our customers, while scanning for a chance to kick off the organization's development. That development opportunity came a year ago to the detriment of one of our rivals."

Gathering up the bankrupt organization, divine Inc., from the sale piece was the simple part; then came the reconciliation of the two organizations. "The procedure was serious and debilitating," says Fasciano, who notes four keys to their prosperity:

- Customer maintenance. "I for one talked with 150 clients inside of the initial couple of weeks of fulfilling the arrangement, and I met with 45 customers around the world in the initial six months," notes Fasciano. They've held 95 percent of the heavenly Inc. client base.
- Staff maintenance. Fasciano rehired the best and brightest of perfect's staff.
- Melding innovations. "One reason I was so sure about this procurement was the two item architectures were fundamentally the same," says Fasciano. This took into consideration a smooth mix of the two advances.
- Focus. "Perhaps the most compelling motivation this obtaining has worked so well is the center that FatWire has conveyed to a disregarded item," says Fasciano.

FatWire's securing of celestial in 2003 developed its client base from 50 to 400, and the organization grew 150 percent, from $6 million to $15 million. Fasciano expects no under $25 million in deals this year.

9. Grow all around. Not just did FatWire develop as far as clients and deals, it additionally experienced worldwide development basically as a consequence of incorporating the best of the celestial and FatWire innovations. "FatWire at long last has universal span we've built up new workplaces in the United Kingdom, France, Italy, Spain, Holland, Germany, China, Japan and Singapore," says Fasciano. This expanded piece of the overall industry is the thing that will permit FatWire to acknowledge managed development.

However, you don't have to gain another business to grow all around. You simply need to prime your offering for a universal market the way FatWire was prepared after the joining of its advancements with divine's.

You'll additionally require a remote wholesaler who'll convey a stock of your item and exchange it in their household markets. You can find outside wholesalers by scouring your city or state for a remote organization with a U.S. delegate. Exchange bunches, remote councils of trade in the United States, and branches of American assemblies of business in outside nations are additionally great spots to discover merchants you can work with.

10. Grow to the Internet. "Charge Gates said that before the end of 2002, there will be just two sorts of organizations: those with an Internet vicinity, and those with no business by any stretch of the imagination," notes Sally Falkow a Pasadena, California, Web content strategist. "Maybe this is exaggerating the case, however a compelling Web website is turning into a basic piece of business today."

Finding your Web webpage in web index results is key-more than 80 percent of movement comes by means of web indexes, as indicated by Falkow. "As there are currently more than 4 billion Web pages and activity on the Internet duplicates at regular intervals, making your Web website unmistakable is fundamental," she says. "You require each weapon you can get."

Outline and writing computer programs are likewise vital, yet it's your substance that will draw a guest into your site and inspire them to sit tight. Says Falkow, "Assembling a substance methodology in view of client conduct, measuring and following guest click streams, and composing the substance taking into account investigated catchphrases will get you superb indexed lists and address the issues and meet the needs of your visitors.

Printed in the United States
By Bookmasters